MONINO
The Russian Air Force Museum

MONINO

The Russian Air Force Museum

A pictorial look at Moscow's unique collection
of aircraft from the former Soviet Union

Colin W. Prentice

Airlife
England

Acknowledgments

The author would like to thank
Maris Multimedia (publishers of the
Wings Series of CD-ROM warplane
encyclopedias) for all their help in
the preparation of this book

First published 1997
by Airlife Publishing Ltd

British Library Cataloguing-in-Publication Data
 A catalogue record for this book
 is available from the British Library

ISBN 1 85310 898 7

Printed in Hong Kong

Airlife Publishing Ltd

101 Longden Road, Shrewsbury SY3 9EB, England

Introduction

The Russian Air Force Museum is housed within the grounds of the Yuri Gagarin Air Force Academy at Monino, a small town on the outskirts of Moscow.

Until recent times this unique collection of aircraft and artifacts was largely unseen, even by Russians. However, since the thaw in the Cold War it has become more accessible and its host of interesting inmates are now regularly seen by Russian and foreign visitors alike. That said, it is unlike any American or European aviation museum. Various 'permissions' and paperwork are still needed before one is allowed to wander around and take photographs, especially inside the hangars.

There are some 150 aircraft on charge at the museum, and about 100 are on display at any one time. Airframes range from fragile World War One types to the latest fighter prototypes from the Design Bureaux. Within the grounds both civil airliners and military fighters are to be seen, often sitting side-by-side in a rather unorganised display layout. As well as fighters and airliners there are bombers, trainers, helicopters, experimental aircraft, and even gliders and light aircraft.

My first visit to Monino was in mid-November 1994. The temperature outside was a chilling -13°C and my pen as well as my camera refused to work in such conditions, even inside the hangars! The same was not to be said for my little 75-year-old guide, who had been a 'Shturmovik' ground crewman during the Russian attack on Berlin in the Second World War (known by the Russians as the Great Patriotic War).

On my second visit the temperature was a stifling +28°C. Monino is a place of stark contrasts, and the airframes residing here suffer greatly from the harsh weather conditions and the lack of funds for preservation and restoration. In the past couple of years, however, much work has been done and the whole place is looking a lot tidier.

Monino is not only a resting place for tired aircraft. The meagre facilities house a large display of models, photographs, artwork and exhibitions showing the achievements of the once vast Soviet Socialist Republic and its aviators and designers. There is also a display of many old aero engines and weapons. It is a very special place for anyone with even a passing interest in aircraft or aviation.

Make your first visit there through the pages of this book, then plan to go in person at the first opportunity and experience the atmosphere of this amazing collection for yourself.

Colin W. Prentice

Main: A real monster of a helicopter is the first aircraft you meet as you enter the outdoor compound. The giant record-breaking, twin-rotor Mil-V12 towers above an Su-35 prototype, a recent addition to the long line of Sukhoi types represented here.

Below: The massive, ghostly shape of the V-12, covered in snow, stands like a protective parent over a 1936 Tupolev SB 2 'Speed Bomber' which is dwarfed by the helicopter's presence.

The V-12 has two Mi-6 engines and rotors. Its lifting capacity exceeded that of the An-22 and the Il-76. This example was taken to a height of 2,255m with a weight of 40,204.5kg in 1969. The project was abandoned because the Mi-26 'Halo' proved to be far superior.

Left: Close to the faded paintwork on the nose of the huge V-12, one gains the impression of looking up at an ageing VTOL 'jumbo jet'.

Above: One of the enormous twin rotorheads on this amazing giant Russian helicopter.

Above: East meets West. The sign at the start of the outside display area separates the Soviet SB 2 bomber and the perhaps more familiar shape of a North American B-25 Mitchell. The B-25 was used in large numbers by the Soviet Union during the Great Patriotic War.

Left: The Tupolev SB 2 of 1936 served in Spain, where it outpaced even the opposing fighters. Its only real drawback was that it caught fire easily when hit in combat.

Below: Monino's example seems to fare well, considering the years of outside display in all weathers.

Above: This fresh looking B-25, resplendent in Second World War Russian markings, is a recent addition to the museum aircraft display.

Right: A line-up of some of the outdoor World War Two aircraft types basking in the welcome summer sun.

Below: Thousands of B-25s were used to good effect by Russian forces during the war with Germany.

Production of the Ilyushin DB-3 began in 1936. It went through various stages of development, and from March 1942 was redesignated Il-4. Total production exceeded 5,250 aircraft.

Another American Lend-Lease bomber from the Great Patriotic War is the Douglas A-20 Boston. On the author's first visit this aircraft was inside the pre-war hangar, but now the somewhat battered warbird squats on the grass with other ageing airframes that would fare better if given the protection of a hangar.

Another wartime design which underwent a great deal of development was the Tu-2 series. The first example flew in early 1942. This aircraft was designed by Andrei Tupolev while he was in captivity. He was later awarded the First Order of Lenin for his work.

No it is not a Boeing B-29 – it is a
Tu-4 'Bull'. During the war some
B-29s were stranded in Russia and
the Soviets were quick to copy the
design. They made alterations to suit
their technology, put the resulting
machine into production and the
result was the Tu-4.

Right: The Tu-4 basks in the +28°C noonday sunshine in May 1996.

Below: Here the huge B-29 'lookalike' sits in the snow in November 1994. The outside temperature was -13°C. They say it gets colder in the winter!

Opposite page: The signage at the museum is a little basic compared with western signs, but if you can read Cyrillic it does the job.

Ту-4

ДАЛЬНИЙ
ТЯЖЕЛЫЙ
БОМБАРДИРОВЩИК
А.Н. ТУПОЛЕВА

Год выпуска 1947

Двигатели АШ-73 тк четыре с мощностью
по 2400 л.с. А.Д. Швецова.

Экипаж	11 чел.
Вес взлетный	63300 кг
Скорость полета	558 км/час
Потолок самолета	11200 м
Дальность полета	5680 км
Бомбовая нагрузка	8000 кг
Вооружение	10 пушек
	калибра 23 мм.

Самолет испытан Н.С. Рыбко, М.Л. Галлаем,
А.Г. Васильченко.

Ту-4 применялся как носитель и заправщик.

Left and below: A civilian version of the Lisunov Li-2 'Cab', registered CCCP93914, rests on the grass in the transport section of the Monino compound. The Li-2 was a licence-built copy of the ubiquitous Douglas DC-3 Dakota. Though it looks like a 'Dak' it is really quite a different aeroplane.

Right and below: The military version of the Li-2 on display at Monino clearly shows the turret above the flaky green paintwork and the square windows. A third Li-2 (wreck) has now been removed from the site.

Probably the most famous Second World War Russian fighter-bomber, the Ilyushin Il-2 Shturmovik is represented at Monino. It resides in the World War Two hangar, along with other famous fighters of the period. Illustrated on this page and top opposite is the similar Il-10M 'Beast', which was the penultimate development of this famous fighter family. The aircraft at Monino was used to train Il-28 'Beagle' gunners in the 1950s.

Below: A replacement for the Li-2 (DC-3) was the Ilyushin Il-12. Development was begun in 1943, and the first flight of the new design was in August 1945. The Il-12 was in Aeroflot service from mid-1947. The Monino example is a military version, the Il-12 'Coach'.

The pathway leading between the Second World War aircraft on the right and the Sukhoi line-up on the left leads to some modern MiGs and eventually to the civil and transport aircraft parked in the field behind the main outdoor display area at Monino.

Left: An Su-7B 'Fitter' starts the line-up of Sukhoi fighters set against a backdrop of tall trees.

Right: This Su-7BM has a ski/skid landing-gear. The Soviets believed that in a modern war there would be no airfields left on which to land. How would you fancy landing a fast jet fighter in a field on skis?

Below: An Su-7BKL. This 'Fitter' has both wheels and skids, to cater for changing conditions.

Above: A fairly smart looking Su-9 'Fishpot' with underbelly tanks and underwing missiles.

Right: The Su-11 'Fishpot' is similar to the Su-9 but displays some external pipework on the fuselage.

Below: This Su-17M-3 'Fitter H' is armed to the teeth and makes an interesting study in the noonday spring sunshine.

Above: An Su-15 'Flagon' interceptor shows the change to side intakes and a pointed nose to accommodate the larger antenna of its improved radar.

Above: The Su-24 'Fencer' looks quite modern and in better shape than some of the airframes on display.

Right: The Su-T-10, which served as the Su-27 'Flanker A' interceptor prototype. The T-10 has an ogival wing.

Left: A late 1950s Yakovlev Yak-28B 'Brewer A' two-seat bomber, left out in the cold.

Below: The same machine warming up in the summer sunshine. Derived from the Yak-26, the first supersonic member of the Yak-25 family, the 'Brewer' had new engines in revised nacelles, a wing raised to shoulder height on the fuselage, a tail of increased area and a revised structure to cater for its increased gross weight.

Above: The Yakovlev Yak-27R 'Mangrove' two-seat reconnaissance aircraft was in service all through the 1960s. It had improved afterburning engines in a Yak-27 airframe.

Above: The Antonov An-14 'Clod' was produced in the early 1960s. It had a crew of one and could accommodate seven passengers. In the CIS it is known as the Pchelka or Little Bee.

Right: The state of the old hangars at Monino somehow adds to the atmosphere of the place. It would, however, be nice to see some money spent on improving the site.

Right: Crowded and almost hiding behind a hangar, these three interesting aircraft sit waiting to be discovered. At the back is the Beriev Be-32, a 1970s feederliner that did not catch on first time round. The Be-32 is now being marketed again with an improved specification.

Below: The 1970s Polish-built PZL M-15 'Belphegor' is a rather unconventional twin-boom agricultural aircraft with the unique distinction of being the world's only purely jet-powered biplane.

Below: Another Polish import to the old USSR was the PZL L-29 Delphin jet trainer. This 1960s vintage aircraft, which had the NATO reporting name 'Maya', is seen here nestled beside an Mi-6 'Hook' firefighting helicopter.

Right: Another heavy helicopter is the recently arrived camouflaged example of the Mi-26 'Halo', currently the world's largest operational helicopter.

Below: A white Mil Mi-6 'Hook' sits in the helicopter compound between the restoration hangar and the pre-war hangar. There are currently no fewer than three examples of the Mi-6 at Monino, all of which can be seen on this page.

Above: The standard Russian shipborne anti-submarine helicopter is the Kamov Ka-25 'Hormone'. A typical example in naval markings is to be found in the helicopter compound.

Right: The tiny Kamov Ka-26 'Hoodlum' was a very unusual design. The fuselage pods could be changed to suit different roles. The example at Monino is fitted with an agricultural hopper and is displayed in Aeroflot colours.

Left: Developed from the Mi-6 'Hook', the Mi-10 'Harke' is a huge flying crane. The 'Harke' was first flown in 1960 and is still in service today. Huge loads can be accommodated on a special platform which can be slung between its undercarriage legs.

Below: The Mi-10 rests close to one of two Mi-8 'Hip' helicopter transports on display at Monino.

Above: The old Mil Mi-4 'Hound' is somewhat similar in appearance to the western Sikorsky S-55 or its licence-built British counterpart, the Westland Whirlwind. Designed in the early 1950s, the 'Hound' soldiered on in service until around 1960.

Right: The smaller Mi-2 'Hoplite' was not produced until the early 1960s. Later, production was continued outside Russia by WSK-Swidnik of Poland. More than 5,000 were built, and many variants are in service today.

The large twin-rotor Yakovlev Yak-24 'Horse' is a type seldom seen by westerners. The 'Horse' was an early 1950s design. The Monino example shares a patch of grass with a smaller American twin-rotor design, a Vertol 44.

How did that get there? An American Vertol 44 'flying banana', still in its faded 30-year-old colour scheme, lies behind the Yak-24 'Horse' in the museum's helicopter park.

Below: This Mi-8 'Hip C', painted in the standard Soviet green scheme, is one of a pair of 'Hips' at Monino.

Right: A 'square-nose' Mi-24 'Hind A', the earliest version of the formidable Mil gunship.

Below: The more recognisable 'Hind' shape. This is a later version, the Mi-24P 'Hind E'. The type was used in Afghanistan.

Right: The Tupolev Tu-16 'Badger A' was an early nuclear bomber.

Below: The later Tu-16K 'Badger G' was a maritime aircraft fitted with 'Kingfish' missiles. A really heavyweight missile platform.

Tupolev's Tu-128A 'Fiddler' was a massive interceptor. The development of various versions continued through the Cold War era of the 1960s and 1970s.

First-generation Russian Jets were
basically piston-engine fighter
designs fitted with jet engines. Here
is the Yak-17 'Feather' of 1947.

Of a similarly basic design to the earlier Yak-17 was the Yak-23 'Flora', which took to the skies about a year after the 'Feather' and had a stressed skin.

Above: The Yakovlev Yak-25 'Flashlight', an early Soviet twin-jet bomber, had a distinctive centreline tandem undercarriage arrangement.

Right: A development of the Yak-25 – the Yak-25RV 'Mandrake' was a single-seat ultra-high-altitude reconnaissance aircraft first flown in 1959. Though basically similar to the 'Flashlight', the 'Mandrake' had a new unswept high-aspect-ratio wing and a new powerplant.

Right: Another of the early Russian jet fighters – the Lavochkin La-15 'Fantail'.

Below: The Lavochkin La-250 was an experimental jet used for early airborne missile test launches.

The first of the line, this Mikoyan
and Guryevich – MiG-9 'Fargo' is the
oldest of the famous MiG jet fighters
on display at Monino.

Above: The single-seat MiG-15bis 'Fagot' found fame in the Korean conflict, in jet-versus-jet combat with the North American F-86 Sabre.

Right: The two-seat trainer version is the MiG-15UTI 'Midget'.

Left: The MiG-17 'Fresco' was the next stage of development. It had a revised wing and an enlarged vertical tail among other changes.

Below: Then came the MiG-19 'Farmer'. During the 1950s the MiG fighters were improving constantly and there were numerous variants of this type, which was built in Poland and China.

The MiG-21 'Fishbed', the most famous of MiG fighters, has developed over more than 30 years, the latest MiG-21 upgrade variant being seen at the Paris Air Show in 1995. Monino has a number of MiG-21 variants. Number '92' (at left) has been here for many years, while '48' (below) is a more recent addition.

This MiG-21 was fitted with a scaled down 'Concordski' wing to test the wing design for the supersonic Tupolev Tu-144 airliner, and was designated MiG-21I Analog. It now sits in the shadow of the SST (Supersonic Transport).

There have been many MiG-21 based experimental airframes. This famous 'record breaker', incorrectly marked as E166, is the Ye-152M, intended as a 'heavy fighter' with much greater climb/acceleration than its forebear, but abandoned.

A twin-jet tactical bomber, the Il-28
'Beagle' was active throughout the
1950s.

Above: More up-to-date Russian hardware in the shape of the rugged Sukhoi Su-25 'Frogfoot', a real 'tankbuster'. The Monino example nestles close to the Tu-144 supersonic transport (SST).

Right: Another modern fighting aircraft; the MiG-23 'Flogger'.

Right: The Sukhoi T-61 is very similar to the British Aircraft Corporation TSR2 in configuration. This was effectively the prototype for the Su-24 'Fencer'.

Below: Two recent arrivals to the museum's outside storage area are what appear to be in-service MiG-23 'Flogger' and MiG-25 'Foxbat'. The author was told that the hangar in which they were housed had collapsed and caused a great deal of damage. The CIS has little money for repairs, so they ended up here.

Above: The twin fins and orifices of a MiG-31 'Foxhound', distinguished from the MiG-25 by its twin-wheel main undercarriage units.

Right: This is a MiG-25P 'Foxbat A'. There are one or two 'Foxbats' in the compound.

'04' is a Mig-25 'Foxbat' interceptor.

A comparative view of '202', a
MiG-31 'Foxhound'.

There are three camouflaged Yak-28L 'Brewers' in the storage area at Monino. As evidenced by the condition of these two, they are in various states of repair.

There is also a two-seat trainer variant – the Yak-28U 'Maestro', and this also looks a bit the worse for wear, the pupil's cockpit in the nose being exposed.

The vertical take-off and landing (VTOL) Yak-36 'Freehand' was an early attempt at thrust vectoring. The nose probe is not for refuelling, but has an exhaust bleed nozzle to help control the aircraft while hovering.

There are two examples of the successful VTOL Yak-38 'Forger' at Monino. The one below is an early version and the other (left) is the later Yak-38M. Note the revised undercarriage and the strakes along the top of the forward fuselage, just discernible.

Right: An early Tupolev Tu-95 'Bear A' turboprop-powered bomber dominates the centre of the main field.

Below: This early version of the Myasishchyev M-4 'Bison' four-jet bomber is also a 'mid-field' heavy-weight resident.

There are a number of MiG-29 'Fulcrum' airframes here. The one above is the prototype (MiG-29/901). The other (at right) is a MiG-29K naval variant with a square-section arrester hook between the jet orifices.

Above: MiG Ye 231 (first
MiG-23 prototype 'Flogger'), sits in
the shade of the 'Mail'.

Above: Another 'Flogger' with the number 231. It is believed to be the third prototype MiG-23.

Left: An early Antonov An-12 'Cub' military transport resides in the civil and transport section of the field.

Most of the civil airliner colours at
Monino are, as one would expect,
somewhat faded 'Aeroflot' schemes
like the one worn by this Yak-40
'Codling'.

Above: This three-engined Yak-42 'Clobber' has been waiting on its ramp for a long time.

Right: Less faded but awkwardly parked is this Antonov An-24 'Coke', designed for short-range routes and primitive airstrips.

Left: A very faded Ilyushin Il-18 'Coot' four-turboprop airliner stands at the end of the row in the long grass.

Below: Interesting markings on a Tupolev Tu-104A 'Camel'. Number '46' has a tail code of '8350705'.

The Tu-124 'Cookpot' is a scaled-down version of the Tu-104. This paint scheme looks fairly new compared with other airliners at Monino.

The Tupolev Tu-114 'Cleat' was based on the Tu-95 'Bear'. This enormous turboprop airliner clocked up 32 records in the early 1960s and Monino's example is the record-breaking prototype, named *Rossiya*. It is also the aircraft in which the then prime minister N. Khrushchev flew direct from Moscow to New York on 15 September 1959.

Above: The Tu-114 is a pretty big aeroplane by any standard, and dominates the centre of the civil park.

Left: A close-up of the *Rossiya*'s two starboard NK-12 turboprop engines and their massive eight-bladed contrarotating propellers.

The gigantic Antonov An-22 Antei, NATO reporting name 'Cock', is another enormous transport. This one was named after Antei, the giant son of Poseidon. The project leading to this machine was started back in 1962, and the prototype first flew on 27 February 1965.

Above: Coming down in size a little, here we see the Antonov An-10A 'Cat'. This was basically an extended-fuselage version of the An-10. The series was successful until a string of structural failures led to the type's withdrawal from service in 1973.

Left: Still smaller was the earlier twin-turboprop An-8 'Camp', which served with both the air force and Aeroflot from the mid-1950s. The amazing VVA-14 'Ekranoplan' can be seen in the background.

Ilyushin Il-62 'Classic' CCCP-86670
provides a comparison of this 1960s
four-jet airliner with the much older
Li-2 transport seen behind.

The Russian Tu-144 'Charger' SST went into service before Concorde but was withdrawn a short while after and never achieved a commercial success. Monino's example is CCCP-77106, seen here towering over the Sukhoi Su-25 'Frogfoot' close-support aircraft.

The distinctive Myasishchyev M-17
Stratosphera, NATO codename
'Mystic A' (CCCP-17103), has been at
Monino for some time now. It was
designed as a reconnaissance
platform, and first flew in 1982.

Another, more recently arrived M-17 has had an accident. This aircraft, CCCP-17401, was the prototype, later modified to series standard, and is covered with environmentalist slogans. Unfortunately it had its tail booms broken off while being transported slung (badly) under an Mi-26 'Halo' helicopter.

Sadly now a derelict hulk, this Bartini design, the VVA-14, was originally an amphibious aeroplane and was later converted to an 'Ekranoplan' or wing in ground effect vehicle. These strange craft are designed to fly at very high speeds just a few feet above the surface. The VVA-14 is therefore not a conventional aeroplane, but is (or rather was) an 'aircraft' nonetheless. The CIS has many different 'Ekranoplan' types, some working over the Caspian Sea. The example at Monino is the third VVA-14. In faded Aeroflot titles, it was dumped at the museum site after suffering fire damage.

Above: The huge, mainly titanium Sukhoi T-4/100 looked a bit 'down in the mouth' in the winter of 1994. The 'droop snoot' had broken under the weight of ice that had built up, and the nose of this monster was wrapped in canvas and supported by a rickety old stepladder!

Right: Similar in layout to the North American XB-70 Valkyrie, the T-4/100 took nine years to produce. First flown in 1972, this airframe logged ten successful flights before being retired to Monino in 1982.

Above: Looking decidedly happier in the spring of 1996, the T-4/100 has had a 'nose job' and is now back in one piece.

Left: Four huge RD-36-41 engines took the T-4/100 to a speed of almost 2,000 mph. Its fuselage is 146ft long.

Another really big bird crouches next to the T-4/100. This is the giant Myasishchyev M-50 'Bounder'. The M-50 was designed as a supersonic nuclear bomber, but its overall performance was poor. When the XB-70 project was terminated, so was the M-50.

The aircraft flew at the Tushino air show of 1961, and that same aircraft, number '12', is parked in 'flying attitude' at Monino today. This was the only one flown. The 'Bounder' has a fuselage length of 187ft and a wingspan of 121ft. It could travel at Mach 1.2 and had a range of 3,750 miles.

'Out to grass' at Monino is this smart looking Tupolev Tu-22M-0 'Backfire A', one of nine flight prototypes of this swing-wing bomber.

A Cold War warrior in retirement, this Tu-22 'Blinder' supersonic bomber and missile carrier has a distinctive twin-tail-mounted engine layout. The prototype made its maiden flight on 21 June 1958.

Above: An experimental pilotless drone, converted from a Russian 'cruise missile', this aircraft is known as the VR-3.

Right: Beside the VR-3 is 'Product 105-11', an air-launched vehicle used to collect data and test systems for the then future, but now defunct 'Buran' space shuttle programme.

Inside Information

There are three hangars on the Monino complex. The main one houses the entrance and early historical exhibits. This is where you pay for your entry to the museum, and also for 'permission' to photograph the aircraft. This hangar also houses the 'Great Patriotic War' (Second World War) exhibits and aircraft. It is relatively simple to obtain permission to photograph outside, but to obtain permission to photograph inside is another matter. The second hangar houses mostly pre-war aircraft types, and the third is out of bounds to visitors. It is where a lot of the repair, storage and restoration work is done. In here you will find Yak-18s, an An-2 and a few other goodies, if you are very lucky.

On the following pages are shown some of the older aircraft and replicas, as well as some of the few light aircraft and gliders that hang from the roof. Photography inside these old hangars is difficult, and even when permission is granted you are not helped or encouraged at all by those in charge.

In this general view inside the pre-war hangar the age and poor condition of the building and the difficult lighting conditions are evident. These buildings were not designed as museum buildings in which to display aircraft; they are originals, built simply to house the aircraft and afford some protection from the elements. Overhead are the 'Discoplan' glider and a rare indigenous lightplane. On the ground in the centre is a Farman IV 'replica' and behind it an 'out of place' Second World War Su-2 fighter. As well as some old aircraft, more modern gliders, motor gliders and large aviation paintings are also to be found in this hangar.

Igor Sikorsky designed the huge four-engined Ilya Mouromets bomber for use in the First World War. After the war he went to America and continued to design aircraft and especially helicopters. This is a very good replica of the Ilya Mouromets, made for a film.

A closer look at the airworthy
Farman IV 'replica', which exhibits
several conspicuous departures from
the original design. It was on this
type that the first Russian airmen
learned to fly.

Russia's first all-metal aeroplane, the Tupolev ANT-2, had an enclosed cabin for the passengers but an open cockpit for the pilot. This ANT-2bis was powered by a British 100hp Bristol Lucifer three-cylinder radial engine.

A beautiful old Tupolev design, the
ANT-25 replica depicts the record-
breaking 'NO25-1' which M. Gromov
flew from Moscow to California in
July 1937.

During the early days of flight the Russians relied heavily on foreign types. Here, in the almost obligatory green paint, an excellent replica represents the French Voisin LA biplane of 1914.

Another First World War import was the British Sopwith Triplane. Delivered in 1917, this was a formidable fighter and was very much liked by Russian pilots. This sole Russian survivor, N5486, is not as authentic as the example in the RAF Museum in Hendon.

The Polikarpov I-15bis was a 1930s design, but more than 1,000 of these biplane fighters were still in service in late 1941.

The wooden Yak UT-2 two-seat
trainer, of which production began in
1938, was the predecessor to the
metal Yak-18 series of the post-war
era.

The Polikarpov Po-2 was not well
known outside the Soviet Union, but
this 1928 biplane was produced in
large numbers and many variants,
more than 33,000 being built. This
one is still airworthy.

Also on display in this hangar are
some of Russia's balloon baskets and
gondolas, hang gliders and the VTOL
thrust measuring rig (far right),
which looks very similar to the old
British Rolls-Royce 'Flying Bedstead'.

Right: What is this tucked away behind the 'Ilya Mouromets' First World War four-engined bomber? It seems to be some sort of experimental glider, but why is it attached to a large cylindrical tank?

Су-2 Ближний бомбардировщик, разведчик и штурмовик конструкции П. О. Сухого. Год выпуска 1940.

На самолетах Су-2 советские летчики принимали участие в Великой Отечественной войне

This aeroplane should really be in the Second World War hangar. It is a Su-2 short-range bomber of 1940. Note the rear gun turret. It was not a popular aircraft with its crews, and suffered severe attrition. This 'restoration' is mainly a replica.

The Great Patriotic War

The Second World War was hard for all countries that were involved in the conflict. Russia, however, suffered more than all of the rest. Millions of Russians gave their lives in the struggle against Nazi Germany, both in defence of their country and in the subsequent attacks on Germany. The main hangar at Monino houses not only displays of many early Russian aviation achievements such as early aero engines, models, artwork and weapons, but also a small collection of aircraft from the Second World War. The following pages show all of these except for the Il-2 Shturmovik (very similar in appearance to the Il-10 displayed outside) and the Yak-9 fighter (a new-build batch of which are now on the airshow circuit in the USA). Though it is antiquated and by Western standards amateurish and cluttered in its presentations, the Russian Air Force Museum at Monino is a treasure trove for enthusiastic explorers and well worth a visit.

Photography is just as difficult in the Second World War hangar. The exhibits are not very well positioned for 'clean' shots, even if they are taken when the place is closed (Russians like long lunch breaks!) Here is the Lavochkin La-7 allegedly flown by Russia's highest-scoring ace of the war, Ivan N. Kozhedub, though it has three 'Hero of the Soviet Union' decorations and the third was awarded after Kozhedub had stopped flying. The machine was brought to Monino soon after the war's end and became the first permanent aircraft on display here.

A replica of the very streamlined MiG-3 high-altitude fighter sits next to the Lavochkin in the main hangar. The MiG-3 was a good performer at height, but in 1940 the air war was usually fought at much lower altitudes, and sadly this aircraft's low-level performance was not exceptional.

Right: The stumpy, almost cartoon-like Polikarpov I-16 fighter had many faults, but it was the best Russian fighter of the late 1930s. It underwent a great deal of development to improve its performance. This is a replica.

Below: A fairly recent addition to the collection is this restored Bell P-63 Kingcobra, an American type that was used more by the Russians than by the Americans. More than 2,400 were sent to the USSR out of a total production run of 3,303.

Above: Another Po-2 resides in the main hangar. This light bomber variant is also fitted with a machine-gun in the rear seat, though how on earth the occupant twisted round to operate it is puzzling! One of Russia's very few 'home-built' aircraft is suspended from the roof truss in the background.

Left: The later Polikarpov R-5 biplane was first flown in 1928. The Monino example is a composite of two airframes, one having been buried for more than 40 years.

Above: The Petlyakov Pe-2 was the standard twin-engine tactical bomber of the Second World War. This aircraft had the NATO reporting name of 'Buck'. More than 1,600 basic Pe-2s were produced. As the war went on the design was developed further.

Right: The exotic Bereznyak-Isayev BI-1 was the first rocket-powered fighter in the world. Its first powered flight was made in mid-1942. There were six active prototypes, but the type never went into production. The aircraft on show is a replica.

Aircraft on display

A-20 Boston	Box	Mi-2	Hoplite	Su-35	(proto)
An-8	Camp	Mi-4	Hound	Sikorsky	
An-10a	Cat	Mi-6 (x3)	Hook	'Ilya Mouromets' (rep)	
An-12	Cub	Mi-8 (x2)	Hip	Tu-2	Bat
An-14	Clod	Mi-10	Harke	Tu-4	Bull
An-22	Cock	Mi-V12	Homer	Tu-16 (x2)	Badger
An-24	Coke	Mi-24 (x2)	Hind	Tu-22	Blinder
ANT-2		MiG-3 (rep)		Tu-22m	Backfire
ANT-25RD		MiG-9	Fargo	Tu-28	Fiddler
ANT-40		MiG-15bis	Fagot	Tu-104	Camel
Beriev Be-12	Mail	MiG-15uti	Midget	Tu-114	Cleat
Beriev Be-32		MiG-17	Fresco	Tu-124	Cookpot
BI-1		MiG-19	Farmer	Tu-144 (SST)	Charger
Boeing V-44		MiG-21 (x2)	Fishbed	Turbolyet 'O'	
B-25 Mitchell		MiG-21 I (exp)		Ut-2	Mink
DB-3	Bob	MiG Ye152M (exp)		Voisin	(rep)
Discoplan (exp glider)		MiG-23 (x2)	Flogger	VVA-14 (Ekranoplan)	
Farman IV (rep)		MiG-25 (x2)	Foxbat	Yak-9	Frank
Il-2 Shturmovik		MiG-29 (x2)	Fulcrum	Yak-17	Feather
Il-10	Beast	MiG-31	Foxhound	Yak-23	Flora
Il-12	Coach	M-15 (PZL)	Belphegor	Yak-24	Horse
Il-14	Crate	Pe-2	Buck	Yak-25	Flashlight
Il-18	Coot	Po-2 (x2)	Mule	Yak-25RV	Mandrake
Il-28	Beagle	Po R-5		Yak-28 (x4)	Brewer
Il-62	Classic	P-63 King Cobra		Yak-36	Freehand
Ka-25	Hormone	Product 105		Yak-38 (x2)	Forger
Ka-26	Hoodlum	Sb 2	(Speed Bomber)		
La-7	Fin	Sopwith Triplane		Gliders	
La-15	Fantail	Su-2		Motor gliders	
La-250 (exp)		Su T-6 (x2)	Fencer	Hang gliders	
Li-2 (x2)	Cab	Su T-10	Flanker A	Home builts	
L-29 (PZL)	Delphin	Su-7 (x3)	Fitter	Balloon gondolas	
M-3 (4)	Bison	Su-9	Fishpot		
M-17	Mystic A	Su-11	Fishpot	Engines	
M-50	Bounder	Su-15	Flagon	Weapons	
M-55	Mystic B	Su-17	Fitter H	Munitions	
		Su-24	Fencer	Artwork	
		Su-25	Frogfoot	Models	
		Su-27	Flanker B		

the author

Colin W. Prentice has been 'plane crazy' all his life, progressing from being an eight-year-old 'spotter' at Southend Airport in Essex to the current producer of the Maris Multimedia/Discovery 'Wings' series of CD-ROM encyclopaedias. Although many of his designs and photographs have been published in the past, this is his first book.

A graphic designer for many years before becoming professionally involved in aviation multimedia projects, Colin produced the layout, photography, research, text and artwork for this book on the aircraft at the Russian Air Force Museum, Monino, Moscow. He is 49 years old, and he and his wife have seven children and eleven grandchildren.

Special thanks to the three 'Maris Muskovites' above.